Soccer Training:

A Step-by-Step Guide on 14 Topics for Intelligent Soccer Players, Coaches, and Parents

Dylan Joseph

Soccer Training: A Step-by-Step Guide on 14 Topics for Intelligent Soccer Players, Coaches, and Parents

By: Dylan Joseph

Bonus!

Wouldn't it be nice to have the steps in this book on an easy 1-page printout for you to take to the field? Well, here is your chance!

Go to this Link for an **Instant** 1-Page Printout: UnderstandSoccer.com/free-printout.

This FREE guide is simply a "Thank You" for purchasing this book. This 1-page printout will ensure that the knowledge you obtain from this book makes it to the field.

Soccer Training:
A Step-by-Step Guide on 14 Topics for Intelligent
Soccer Players, Coaches, and Parents
All rights reserved
May 14, 2018
Copyright ©2018 Understand, LLC
Dylan@UnderstandSoccer.com
Credit: Cover Design by Jihyeon Joung
Credit: Back Cover Photo by Steve Gabrail of
Studio 41 Photography
Printed in the United States of America

Table of Contents

About the Author

There I was, a soccer player who had difficulties scoring. I wanted to be the best on the field but lacked the confidence and know-how to make my goal a reality. Every day, I dreamed about improving, but the average coaching and my lack of knowledge only left me feeling alone and like I couldn't attain my goal. I was a quiet player and my performance often went unnoticed.

This all changed after my junior year on the Varsity soccer team of one of the largest high schools in the state. During the team and parent banquet at the end of the season, my coach decided to say something nice about each player. When it came to my turn to receive praise, the only thing he came up with was that I had scored two goals that season even though it was against a lousy team, so they didn't really count...

It was a very painful statement that after the 20+ game season, all that could be said of my efforts were two goals that didn't count. Since that moment, I have been forever changed considering one of my greatest fears came true; I was called out in front of my family and friends. Because of that, I got serious. With a new soccer mentor, I focused on the training necessary to obtain the skills to build my confidence and become the goal scorer I always dreamed of being. The next season, after just a few months, I found myself moved up to the starting position of center midfielder and scored my first goal of the 26 game season in only the third game.

I kept up the additional training led by a proven goal scorer to build my knowledge. Fast forward to present day and as a result of the work and focus on the necessary skills, I figured out how to become a goal scorer who averages about two goals and an assist per game, all because of an increase in my understanding of how to play soccer. I was able to take my game from bench-warmer who got called out in front of everybody to the most confident player on the field.

Currently, I am a soccer trainer in Michigan working for Next Level Training. I advanced through their rigorous program as a soccer player and was hired as a trainer. This program has allowed me to guide world-class soccer players for over a decade. I train soccer players in formats ranging from one-hour classes to weeklong camps and from instructing groups of 30 soccer players all the way down to working one-on-one with individuals looking to play for the United States National Team. If you live in the metro Detroit area and want to be the best player in the league, Next Level Training is for you. Learn more at Next-LevelTraining.com. Please leave a review for this book at the end.

Additional Books by the Author that are Available on Amazon:

Soccer Shooting & Finishing: A Step-by-Step Guide on How to Score

Soccer Dribbling & Foot Skills: A Step-by-Step Guide on How to Dribble Past the Other Team

Soccer Passing & Receiving: A Step-by-Step Guide on How to Work with Your Teammates

Dedication

This book is dedicated to all the soccer players, coaches, and parents who are reading this book to improve their knowledge and to strengthen others around them. Whether it be for yourself, your team, or your child, growing to help others and yourself develop is exceptionally noble and speaks volumes to the person you are.

Also, this book is dedicated to my wife. She has supported me on this journey to provide you with the information to improve your understanding of soccer. Because of her continued support and love throughout the writing of this book, she has helped me tremendously to bring this book to you.

Preface

This book was written to change the way players think about and play the game of soccer. I struggled for years with sub-average performances as a defender, defensive center midfielder, and outside midfielder. I was often placed in these positions because I could not score. Due to immaturity, I did not like others correcting my form since I knew it needed considerable improvement, so I would take it personally when someone gave me feedback. I realized that this was limiting my ability to become the player that I wanted to be.

Therefore, I sought out the knowledge that allowed me to score multiple goals a game, defend correctly, pass with excellent form, etc. As a result of this success, I could not help but share my understanding of the game to other players who are looking to improve, parents who want to boost their child's confidence on the field, and coaches who want to be viewed as outstanding by all of their players and their players' parents. Though I train players individually and in small groups, I know that writing the information down in a book will allow it to reach more eyes, build more confidence, and make a significant impact on the world.

Soccer is such a fun and exciting sport for some and I want it to be that way for all. In this book's 14 insightful chapters, many of the crucial areas of soccer are broken down in a way that is easily understood. I am a fan of learning from books and even YouTube videos on how to become better at soccer. I find, however, that there is typically no logical order on how the videos are created, so viewers of the video obtain bits and pieces of knowledge here and there, but do not understand the steps on how to put the pieces together. That is where this book comes in: To fill in those voids in the understanding of how to improve playing, parenting, and coaching in soccer.

This book dives deep into the important topics of soccer. Though the correct form and tactics are extremely helpful in ensuring the ball ends up in the opponent's net, you also need a strong mindset to improve on any weaknesses, solidify your strengths, and implement many tips, tricks, tweaks, and techniques to become the person on your team that consistently scores.

This book will help you become the most admired player on your team. Understand that changing up one or two things may help you become better, but once you start implementing most, if not all of the techniques described in this book, you will see a significant improvement in your performance on the field. The knowledge in this book is only helpful when applied. Therefore, apply it to be sure you are scoring 10X more goals each season, which will lead to several more wins every season for your team. For any words that you are unsure of the meaning, please reference the glossary in the back of the book.

INDIVIDUAL SOCCER PLAYER'S PYRAMID

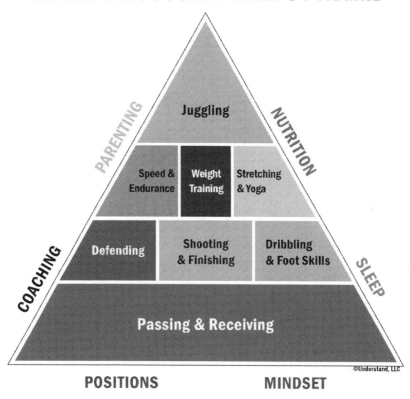

If you are looking to improve your skills, your child's confidence, or your players' abilities, it is essential to understand where this book fits into the bigger picture of developing a soccer player. In the image above, you can see that the most critical field-specific things to work on are at the base of the Individual Soccer Player's Pyramid. Note: A team's pyramid may look slightly different based on the tactics the players can handle and the approach the coach decides to use for games. The pyramid is a quality outline when you are looking to improve an individual soccer player's game. All of the elements in the pyramid and the items surrounding it play a meaningful part in becoming a better player, but certain things should be read and mastered first before moving on to other topics.

You will notice that passing & receiving is at the foundation of the pyramid because if you can receive a pass and make a pass in soccer, you will be a useful teammate. Though you may not be the one that is consistently scoring, the person that is dispossessing the other team, or the player that can dribble through several opponents, you will have the fundamental tools needed to play the sport and contribute to your team.

As you move one layer up, you find yourself with a decision to make on how to progress. Specifically, the pyramid is created with you in mind because each soccer player and each soccer position has different needs. Therefore, your choice regarding which path to take first is dictated by the position you play and more importantly, by the position that you want to play. In soccer and life, just because you are in a particular spot, position, or even a job, it does not mean that you have to stay there forever if that is not your choice. However, it is not recommended to refuse playing a position if you are not in the exact role you want. It takes time to develop the skills that will allow you to make a shift from one position to another.

If you are a forward or if you want to become one, then consider your route on the second layer of the pyramid to start with shooting & finishing. As your abilities to shoot increase, your coach will notice your new finishing skills and be more likely to move you up the field if you are not a forward already. Be sure to communicate to the coach that you desire to be moved up the field to a more offensive position, which will increase your chances as well. If you are already a forward, then dive deep into this topic to ensure you become the leading scorer on your team and in the entire league. Notice that shooting & finishing is considered less critical than passing & receiving because you have to pass the ball up the field before you can take a shot on net.

Otherwise, you can start by progressing to dribbling & foot skills from passing & receiving because the proper technique is crucial to dribble the ball well. It is often necessary for a soccer player to use a skill to protect the ball from the other team or to advance the ball up the field to place their team in a favorable situation to score. The selection of this route is often taken first by midfielders and occasionally by forwards.

Defending is another option of how you can proceed from passing & receiving. Being able to keep the other team off the scoreboard is not an easy task. Developing a defender's mindset, learning which way to push a forward, understanding how to position your body, knowing when to foul, and using the correct form for headers is critical to a defender on the back line looking to prevent goals.

Finish all three areas in the second layer of the pyramid before progressing up the pyramid. Dribbling and defending the ball (not just shooting) are useful for an attacker, shooting and defending (not just dribbling) are helpful for a midfielder, while shooting and dribbling (not just defending) are helpful for a defender. Having a well-rounded knowledge of the skills needed for the different positions is important for all soccer players. It is especially essential for those soccer players looking to change positions in the future. Shooting & finishing, dribbling & foot skills, and defending are oftentimes more beneficial for soccer players to learn first than the next tier of the pyramid, so focus on these before spending time on areas higher up in the pyramid. In addition, reading about each of these areas will help you to understand what your opponent wants to do as well.

Once you have improved your skills at the 1st and 2nd tiers of the pyramid, move upwards to fitness. As you practice everything below this category on the pyramid, your fitness and strength will naturally increase. It is difficult to go through a passing/dribbling/finishing drill for a few minutes without being out of breath. Performing the technical drills allows soccer players to increase their fitness naturally. This reduces the need to focus exclusively on running for fitness. Coming from a soccer player and trainer (someone with a view from both sides), I know that a constant focus on running is not as fulfilling and does not create long-lasting improvements. Whereas, emphasizing the shooting capabilities, foot skills, and defending knowledge of a soccer player does create long-lasting change. Often, the coaches that focus on running their players in practice are the coaches that care to improve their team but have limited knowledge of many of the soccer-specific topics that would quickly increase their players' abilities. Not only does fitness in soccer include your endurance, but it also addresses your ability to run with agility and speed, develop strength and power, while improving your flexibility through stretching and yoga to become a well-rounded soccer player.

Similarly to the tier below it, you should focus on the fitness areas that will help you specifically, while keeping all of the topics in mind. For example, you may be a smaller soccer player that could use some size. Then, you would emphasize weight training and gain the muscle to avoid being pushed off the ball. However, you would still want to stretch before and after a lifting workout or soccer practice/game to ensure that you stay limber and flexible, so that you can recover quickly and avoid injuries.

Maybe you are a soccer player in your 20s, 30s, or 40s. Then, emphasizing your flexibility and practicing a bit of yoga would do a world of good to ensure you keep playing soccer for many more years. However, doing a few sets of push-ups, pull-ups, squats, lunges, sit-ups, etc. per week will help you maintain or gain a desirable physique.

Furthermore, you could be in the prime of your career in high school, college, or at a pro level, which would mean that obtaining the speed and endurance to run for 90+ minutes is the most essential key to continue pursuing your soccer aspirations.

Finally, we travel to the top of the pyramid, which includes juggling. Juggling the soccer ball is something fun to practice in your own free time away from the field or when you are standing in line and waiting to start a drill. It will certainly help with your first touch, but there are more important things to develop during an individual's or team's practice. A general recommendation is that when you can juggle the ball 50 times in a row or more with either of your feet, continuing to work on juggling will not provide huge increases in your performance. Therefore, use juggling as a way to fill otherwise unproductive time in training or during free time to more quickly become a great soccer player.

The last portion of the pyramid are the areas that surround the pyramid. Though these are not skills and topics that can be addressed by your physical abilities, they each play key roles in rounding out a complete soccer player. For example, having a supportive parent/guardian or two is beneficial for transporting the child to games, providing the equipment needed, the fees for the team, expenses for individual training, and encouragement. Having a quality coach will help the individual learn how their performance and skills fit into the team's big picture.

Sleeping enough is critical to having energy in practices and on game days, in addition to recovering from training and games. Appropriate soccer nutrition will increase the energy and endurance of a soccer player, help the soccer player achieve the ideal physique, and significantly aid in the recovery of the athlete. Understanding soccer positions will help to determine if a specific role is well-suited given your skills. It is important to know that there are additional types of specific positions, not just forwards, midfielders, and defenders. A former or current professional player in the same position as yours can provide you guidance on the requirements of effectively playing that position. Last, but not least, is developing a mindset that leaves you unshakable. This mindset will help you become prepared for game situations, learn how to deal with other players, and be mentally tough enough to not worry about circumstances that you cannot control, such as the type of field you play on, the officiating, or the weather. The pyramid is a great visual aid to consider when choosing what areas to read next as a soccer player, coach, or parent.

Chapter 1

Shooting a Driven Shot

Any action in soccer can be broken down into essential components. The four guidelines of a driven shot in soccer, listed in order to ensure precision, accuracy, and power are:

1. Start diagonal to the ball.
2. Plant a foot away from the ball.
3. On the foot you are striking the ball with, have your toe down and out with your knee facing the target so that you can use the bone of your foot.
4. Follow through, land on your shooting foot, bring your back leg forward, and point your hips where you want the ball to go.

To further understand the rules, consider the following:

1. **Stand at a 45° angle "diagonal" to the ball.** You want to be three or four steps from the ball to begin a running start to the ball because the faster you are moving towards the ball, you will naturally have more power on your shot once you make contact. Comparatively, standing still and trying to strike the ball will reduce the power on your shot. As you stand 45° (diagonal) to the ball, you want your shoulders facing the ball as you approach the ball. Being directly behind the ball when you approach it ensures:

-Your shot is going to be diagonal across the goal's frame, which would result in a missed shot.

-You will have to change the part of your foot that you strike the ball with to have an accurate shot, which makes it so that it will not be a driven shot. It ends up either being a shot with the inside of your foot (a pass shot) or a toe ball/toe blow/toe poke with the toes of your foot.

2. **Run at the ball and plant (with the non-striking leg) one foot away from the ball**. The taller you are, the further you plant away. The smaller you are, the closer you plant to the ball, but for the average person, you will be planting about a foot away. Planting too close to the ball will make it so that you have to change the part of the foot that you are using to strike the ball. Therefore, it will no longer be a driven shot.

Plant too far away from the ball and you will barely be able to reach the ball and will lose nearly all of the power on your shot. Make sure your plant foot is pointing at the portion of the net that you are looking to place the ball with your shot.

3. Fully contract your leg back to bring your foot behind your body. Bending at the knee and the hip allows you to bring your foot back correctly. **If you only bend at the knee or the hip, you will lose a lot of muscle on the shot and therefore a lot of power.** Bending at the knee allows your quadriceps to be engaged when striking the ball. Bending at the hip allows your hip flexor to be involved in the shot. Put them together and you will have a much harder shot. As you begin to drive your leg through the ball for a shot forcibly, make sure that your toe is down and out, and your knee is facing the target. Keep in mind that the target is not the net.

The target is where the goalie is not in the net. Therefore, do not only point your knee at the net. Look to determine the portion of the net towards which you are striking the ball. Turning your knee so that it is facing out instead of towards the target will make it so that you are shooting the ball with the inside of your foot. For many soccer players, this tends to be more accurate because it is very close to the form of passing. However, because the inside of your foot is softer than the hardest portion of your foot that you use when you strike the ball with your toe down and out, it makes it so that you lose a lot of power on your shot.

If you practice exclusively with your toe facing down and out, taking inside of the foot shots will not be comfortable. Being most comfortable with driven shots is for the best because the inside of the foot shots are not nearly as powerful and much easier to defend by a goalkeeper versus a driven shot if they are both placed in the same spot on the net. **As your leg follows through the ball, use the bone of your foot (the hardest portion of your foot where the laces meet the leather towards the inside of your foot) to strike the ball.** If you are looking for more power on your shot, striking the ball with the hardest portion of your foot will ensure there is power.

Think of the bone of your foot almost as if it is a baseball "bat," whereas further along your foot (towards your toes) is more like a "broom." A "bat" is harder than a "broom," so using the "bat" to hit the ball will give you more power than using the "broom." However, there is a time to use both portions of the top of your foot. If you are trying to loft the ball over a wall or a defender, striking the ball with the bone/"bat" of your foot will likely send it flying over the net or over the person, which you are trying to loft the ball too. Striking the ball towards the top of your toes (the "broom") will allow the ball to go over the wall or defender, but then dip down because it will not have as much power.

4. After striking the ball, follow through with your leg to generate more power and accuracy on your shot. Follow through with the opposite leg as well. **Therefore, after you strike the ball, you will be landing past the spot on the field from which you struck the ball initially.** Essentially, strike the ball and follow through to a spot past where the ball was before you kicked the ball. Following through is similar if you were to "accidentally" throw a punch. You would not throw the punch with just your arm. You would use your entire body, including your hips, to turn at the waist to extend your arm as you throw the punch to have more power. You generate your power for nearly all athletic moves through your hips.

Similarly, **you do not want to strike the ball with just your leg. You want to strike it using your leg and your entire body.** The bone/"bat" of your foot is the portion that makes contact with the ball. Then, you will follow through your shot, land past the ball, and bring your planting leg forward while pointing your hips at your target. Again, the target is the portion of the net where the goalie is not located. Bringing your back leg/planting leg forward is key to easily allow you to turn your hips towards the portion of the net you want the ball to travel. Learn more about how to score in the second book in the series – *Soccer Shooting & Finishing: A Step-by-Step Guide on How to Score.*

Parenting Tip:

-**Visualizing your shot** (or anything you will do in soccer or in life) before you take it is about 70-80% as effective as actually having taken a practice shot from that same spot.

Coaching Tip:

-Keeping your head down while you strike the ball keeps your chest over the ball, keeps your form together for a more accurate shot, and reduces the chance that the ball will go flying over the net. Personally, I know it is tough to keep your head down. I too like to watch all my shots go in, **but lifting your head will worsen your form**. Would you rather view all of your goals and have less of them or be the top scorer on the team, but only see a few of your goals?

Chapter 2

Finishing

You likely noticed that there was a chapter already on shooting. This section is about making sure you do not shoot just to shoot. It is to ensure that your shots result in goals for your team. In the previous chapter, we went over how to strike a ball using the bone of your foot, to have a very driven and powerful shot. Now, we will discuss tactics to increase the probability that your well-driven shot goes in the net. **To be a good finisher, make sure that you aggressively push the ball and explode away with the ball after doing a skill.** There are three essential reasons for this:

1. **It provides space between you and the defender.** Therefore, you will have slightly more time to pick your head up to see where the goalie is not to aim your shot.

2. If you accelerate after pushing the ball, you will have more speed running to the ball. **If you have more speed running to the ball, you are naturally going to have a more powerful shot.** For example, imagine you are standing still and you strike a shot with your foot planted next to the ball versus having a good three to four step run up on the ball. You can kick it a lot further with a run up when your

momentum, your body, and your hips can help strike through the ball.

3. **An aggressive push past the defender gets you closer to the net.** The closer you are to the net, the more accurate you will be as the net becomes bigger. Additionally, being closer to the net, the goalie is going to have less time to react to stop your shot.

Pushing the ball past a defender is best suited for when you have just performed a foot skill. You push the ball with the outside portion of your laces about 5-7 yards behind the defender. Please keep in mind faster players can afford to push the ball further than slower players. Also, a 5-7 yard push works great when you are going against only one defender, but if there is another defender behind the defender you just used a foot skill on, then you want to use a smaller push that will travel 2-3 yards. This will help avoid you pushing the ball into the supporting defender's feet.

It is critical that you go into a game with the mindset that you will be taking shots. **If your current mindset has you a little bit scared to shoot, you are likely not going to be a good finisher.** You have to have confidence in yourself, so as you read this book and implement the skills, tips, and tricks this book mentions, you will gain confidence in your striking and will consider yourself a finisher. You do not always have to hit the ball with the bone of your foot for it to be a good shot. When you watch professional players, they will use a driven shot, a shot with passing form, a toe-poke, and even use the outside of their foot.

Using all portions of your foot will help trick your defenders. **Toe-pokes allow you to have a lot of power with very little leg motion.** By just extending your knee and hitting the ball with your toe, most defenders are not prepared for an attacker to kick the ball with his or her toe. Most players have been trained from a very young age that kicking a ball with their toe is not a proper way to kick the ball. However, if you watch Ronaldo and Ronaldinho, you will notice they use a toe-poke on occasion because it brings an element of surprise. Also, you will even find soccer players using the outside of their foot to strike the ball. Shooting with the outside of your foot is a more technical way to fire a shot, but also **brings an element of surprise as most defenders do not expect you to strike a ball using the outside laces of your shooting foot.**

Furthermore, you do not have to be entirely past the defender to take a shot. **All you need is just a little bit of space to create a shot that is effective and on target.** If the defender has been covering you well during the game, shooting into their shins/ankles is not going to help your team at all, but keep in mind that you miss 100% of the shots that you do not take. It is much more important for a soccer team to try to increase the volume of its shots because more shots result in more chances for the ball to go in.

Let us play out a situation; a team that takes 30 shots in a game versus a team that takes five really good shots. The team that takes 30 shots is still probably going to win because there are more opportunities for the goalie to accidentally make a mistake, for the shooting team to have a lucky shot, or for the goalie to give up a rebound and a teammate places the rebound into the back of the net.

Parenting Tip:

-Make sure to emphasize that shooting the ball over the net is absolutely unacceptable. **A shot over the net is a waste of a chance.** Yes, the glamour goals (the ESPN Top 10 highlight plays) are generally the shots that go perfectly upper-90 past the goalkeeper. However, in reality, unless you are taking a free kick, those are very low probability shots.

You want to be striking high probability shots that increase your team's ability to score and these are shots that are low or on the ground. Frequently, the shots will be towards the far post. These are great because it is difficult for the goalie to travel to the ground to stop a shot that is low to the ground. If he or she can reach the ball, usually there will be a rebound that ends up in the middle of the 18-yard box. As long as your team has someone positioned to find rebounds, they will be shooting on a mostly empty net. Shooting the ball over the net wastes your team's opportunity to score. It is not about taking more shots; it is about taking more shots on target.

Coaching Tip:

-It is important to realize that taking **shots from 35 yards out have a very low probability of going in**. If your team has 30 shots in a game and they are all from 35 yards out, there is a pretty good chance you are not going to score a single one. Make sure your shots are reasonable. You want more of them, but do not be afraid to take a lot of shots at the top of the 18-yard box. It will ensure you have many opportunities to score or at least create a rebound, which another teammate can place in the net.

Chapter 3

Being Coachable

As an athlete, you want to make sure that you are really approachable and very coachable. Having the ability to be coached ensures that you will be able to absorb the knowledge that your coaches tell you. We like to think that we know everything, but being open to other people's opinions, ideas, and words of wisdom make it so that we are even more knowledgeable and start approaching the state of "knowing everything." Granted, this is an unachievable goal, as it is impossible to know everything, but being coachable will enable you to learn more than another athlete that has a fixed mindset. **In sports and in life, it is critical to have a growth mindset where you are continually seeking out new information**, as well as learning new skills, tips, and tricks about all of the endeavors in your life that you believe to be significant. Not only is this important on the field, but in the classroom and at home as well.

Though not in the same sport, Michael Jordan, the famous basketball player, was referenced by other players and coaches as being the most coachable player that they have ever played with or coached. He was willing to listen to everyone to find little nuggets and tidbits of information that were useful that he adopted to improve his game. However, keep in mind that even though **everyone may have an**

opinion, not everyone is worth listening to or qualified to give advice. Have an initial conversation with that person or coach to see if they are someone from which you should be learning. Some people want to put in their "two cents," but it is not worth anything more than that.

Something that Michael Jordan did was that he sought out other star players and great coaches to find ways to improve his game. He used the knowledge and a second-to-none work-ethic to become one of the best basketball players of all time. Notice what was said, which is a key to knowledge - learning only to learn will make you a fool. You must apply what you have learned. You have to take action! You will learn just as much from doing as you will from reading a book or listening to a coach. **However, if you know "everything," but have never applied it, then technically you may understand it, but you do not know it until you can do it consistently.**

Therefore, in a practice or a game, anytime the coach gives a piece of information to the entire group or you specifically, **make sure to thank them for the feedback even if they are doing it in a mean way.** If you want the coach to know that you are coachable because you care so much about being a better player, take action on what they say immediately. This mindset of immediate action will be very obvious to coaches and show them that you are open to their feedback. Also, remember that it is just feedback, not a personal attack against you. It is not that they hate you, are trying to tear you down, or want to make you less of a player; it is instead that they care about you and want you to improve rapidly. If you show that you care about their opinions and implement their teachings, they will like you even more. As a result, they will play you even more and you will learn the most possible from them.

Parenting Tip:

-**Use the sandwich technique when giving feedback.** First, give a compliment on something that they are performing well. Keep the praise quick and straightforward, such as "good job approaching the ball diagonally." Then, give feedback and explain why. For example, say "plant your foot further from the ball, which will allow you to turn your toe down and out more." Finally, end with another compliment and explanation like "great job following through; it will ensure you have plenty of power on your shot."

This sandwich method is crucial for helping players that have a fixed mindset. By beginning with a compliment, you will break down any walls they have built up against feedback. By ending with a compliment, you leave them with a good feeling that they are doing most things correctly. By providing feedback in the middle of two compliments, you make sure that they hear your message and that they have positive associations with it. Include explanations for all three to guarantee that your message sticks.

Coaching Tip:

-Make sure anytime you are giving advice, do not attack the player, just address the situation. Discussing the situation is critical because if one of your players does something counterproductive, that is not who they are as a person. That is just the way they performed it in a practice or a game, so correct what they did but avoid offending them personally. What often works for me is to let them know:

-How I have made the same types of mistakes
-Exactly what I did wrong
-What I did to correct it
-The outcome of the changes I made

For example, one question I often ask my trainees is "how old was I when I first learned to use my left foot?" I let them guess and they find out that I was 14 years old. Then, I ask them if that is good or bad. They will tell me that that it is bad and I agree with them. Then, I let them know that I make mistakes too, but because I learned that it is essential to be able to use both feet, I practiced using my left foot for an entire summer. I used it exclusively until I was proficient using it and it was helpful instead of holding me back.

The outcome is that now because I am better dribbling with my right foot than with my left foot, the ball ends up on my left foot after I perform a foot skill. Therefore, I actually score more goals with my left foot than my right foot, all because I took massive action to practice improving a weakness of mine. My outcome is that I score more goals with my left foot than my right foot and that I score more goals overall because I can effectively use both feet. Being able to use both feet results in the defender having a difficult time preventing me from scoring.

Chapter 4

Parenting

As the parent of a soccer player, it is vital that you are continually supportive and reassuring to your child. **Only focusing on the bad aspects of their game and criticizing their performances will just drive them away from the game they love.** This is not advice that you should never give them any feedback on areas to improve, but pick your battles. As they are growing (you will obviously know your son or daughter better than I would), they are still working on developing their self-esteem and their self-confidence.

Constant criticisms will only tear them down and will not build them up in the way that is productive. Some easy things to do are celebrate their successes if they score a goal, make an assist, or help the team achieve their goal of winning a game. **Tell him or her "good job," give him or her a pat on the back, and brag about him or her in front of other people.** However, in situations where they do not do so good, still be supportive of them.

As mentioned previously in the book, use the sandwich technique where you compliment them for something that they are doing well. Give them some feedback on something you noticed that they could improve, but make sure that it indeed is something that must be improved. Frequently, parents will think that their kid is supposed to be doing one thing on the field, whereas the coach has them doing something entirely different. Make sure your communication lines are open as a parent working with your child to help them become a better player. **Having a good relationship and excellent communication with your child will ensure that they bring things up to you.**

For example, my sister played center midfield. Growing up, she started her soccer career in the American Youth Soccer Organization (AYSO). At a younger age than many of her soccer peers, she began using much larger nets, so she had much more experience striking shots that were higher in the air. The nets were a lot bigger and the goalies could not reach most of the spots further up in the net. In fact, she averaged over a goal a game and nearly all of them were shots that went over the goalkeeper. However, after a disappointing loss, her travel soccer coach had told the entire team that he did not want anyone shooting from outside the 18-yard box.

For the next several games, my sister no longer shot from the spots where she scored nearly all of her goals. Therefore, my parents asked her why she was not shooting as she previously had done when she was outside of the 18-yard box. She mentioned to them that the coach told everyone to stop shooting from that far out, so she no longer did it because she wanted to follow the coach's direction.

Then, my parents, who were upset by this information because it was making it so that she was not scoring from the spots that she usually scored from, decided to approach the coach and nicely asked him why he said that to the team. He said "oh my gosh, she is following that advice? I meant that for the other girls on the team because they were trying to shoot the ball like her. All of their shots were going right to the goalkeeper, were not powerful, and not above the goalkeeper to score."

Had my parents not had a good relationship with my sister and the ability to communicate different things that they noticed in a game, my sister would have stopped shooting from outside the 18-yard box for the rest of the season. They had many more games that season and she would not have been taking her usual shots. Therefore, it is critical that you keep the communication lines open with your player and avoid criticisms in most circumstances. Constructive criticism wrapped in compliments works very well. **Rewarding the good produces more good, whereas criticizing the bad often produces more bad.** Focus on what you want and for the most part, let the bad fall by the wayside.

Parenting Tip:

-Be reasonable with coaches. **Be honest with yourself.** If your son or daughter is not the best player on the team, acknowledge it and seek to improve them by increasing their understanding of the game and potentially additional training. The coach is likely doing their best given all the information they have at that time. Keep in mind, though we wish this were not the case, the worse the relationship you have with the coach, the more it will affect your child's positioning and play time. Just as you give your son or daughter compliments, keep in mind that coaches love to hear praise too for things they are doing well.

Coaching Tip:

-As a coach, sometimes you have to deal with unruly parents. Many of us have had parents that thought their kid was an absolute all-star. However, we both know that they probably should not have even come off the bench with their subpar performances. That same parent will be personally offended when you do not play their son or daughter as much as they think is appropriate. **Here, one of the worst things you can do is to tell them that their kid is not good.** You want to be gentle and explain that as a coach, you are trying to have the team to work as well as possible. Mention that their performance has been lacking a little bit in practices, so you reward good results in practices with playing time in games. This statement does multiple things:

1. It lets the parent know that their kid will play if they improve.

2. It gently lets them know that their kid has room for improvement, which makes it easier for a parent to see the need for additional training, courses, and books on how to help their son or daughter improve in the game they love.

3. It makes it so that you do not appear to be the enemy; you just want the best result for the team. If you have one parent that dislikes you and they have some influence with the other parents, you could have a problem where many parents are against you, which destroys the team's chemistry. Remember that this is still your team. You are the coach and you may make some mistakes. You are human and mistakes happen in a game where maybe you should have played someone else and did not.

Perhaps you played someone in an incorrect position versus what would have been better for the team, but you just did not know it at the time. **Therefore, keep in mind that mistakes will occur, but errors should be viewed only as feedback.** Remind yourself that they are just parents letting you know that they are distraught or that they feel something was wrong and it should be improved upon going forward. Be open to the feedback. Do not see the parents as the enemy. See their opinions as opportunities to grow. Improve your ability to communicate as a coach and learn from other people's perspectives because when you watch the game, you only have one set of eyes to view the action.

Wherever you are standing on the sidelines, parents may see other things that you are not able to fully view. If they bring their perspectives up to you, **say "thank you for the feedback"** and that you will surely consider what they said. This ensures that they are on your side and that they are looking out for your best interest. Keep the communication lines open with the parents, so that they want their son or daughter to be on your team and so it does not create voids in the group from parents that are distraught with their child's play time, position, etc.

Chapter 5

Foot Skills

Though there are many skills for a soccer player to develop, having effective foot skills to use in a game that will get you past defenders builds confidence in a soccer player like nothing else. The four essential foot skills are as follows:

1. Feint (also known as a "jab," a "body feint," a "fake," a "fake and take," or a "shoulder drop")
2. Self-Pass (also known as an "L," "la croqueta," or an "Iniesta")
3. Shot Fake
4. Cut

When performing foot skills, it is vital to remember that you are trying to be as quick and as efficient as possible. Whether you like him or not, Lionel Messi is arguably the best dribbler in the world. If you ever watch Lionel Messi play, he does not use very flashy moves such as the scissor, rolls, rainbows, etc. Messi uses skills that enable him to be as quick as possible to travel past the defenders.

Quite honestly, when you watch him, it does not even look like he is using that many skills at all. It seems like he is just running around people on the other team. When you make it look like you are just running past defenders, it is a sign of excellent foot skills. The more in-depth a move is, the more time it takes. **The more time a skill takes, the easier it is for the defender to recover and steal the ball from you or for support to help the defender out in taking the ball from you.**

1. **A "feint" or a "jab" is when you pretend to push the ball in one direction past the defender. However, you purposely miss the ball, then plant with the foot that you just missed the ball with, at which point you push the ball in the other direction past the defender.** It is critically important to make sure to sell this move with your shoulders and hips. This means that you should not only miss the ball with the leg that pretended to push the ball, but also to have your hips and shoulders pointing in the direction you are trying to fake the defender into believing you are traveling.

Use this skill when you are attacking and the defender is back pedaling (jockeying) you. All you are trying to do in this instance is to have the defender to plant a little bit too firmly on one leg because of your skill. If they plant too heavily, it will make it so that they cannot reach very far when you explode past them in the other direction. Two things that seemingly overnight had changed my ability to attack a defender was the knowledge of:

-You do not have to be directly behind the defender to beat the defender. If you are close enough to the net and you create just enough space to shoot, then the skill is considered successful, granted you are taking a decent shot or making a quality pass.

-A skill buys you a little bit of time. A move done correctly results in the defender planting too heavily on one leg or a bit of a flinch from the defender. **However, the real way that you create space with your skill is the acceleration after the skill.** When you watch the likes of Lionel Messi, Neymar, Ronaldo, you notice that after any skill they perform, they explode with speed to run away from the defender.

2. The self-pass, also known as the Iniesta, is nicknamed after the famous Barcelona midfielder and captain Andrés Iniesta. Furthermore, he helped lead the Spanish national team to Euro Cup and World Cup wins. It is nicknamed after him because he uses it so frequently and more than any other player. **The self-pass is simply just a pass from one foot to the other while you are running with the ball.** Imagine you are doing a roll (also known as a rollover), but without your foot going on top of the ball. Instead, the self-pass is an inside of the foot pass with one foot and an inside of the foot push up the field with the other foot. The motion that the ball makes is that of the letter "L" or a reversed "L." The self-pass will help you travel directly behind the defender,

but if you open up the foot that is pushing the ball up the field, you will be able to push the ball diagonal to your body, which will set you up for a driven shot on net.

Use this foot skill in a situation where the defender over commits and instead of jockeying you, they jump in to try and steal the ball. Since they are lunging towards you (and the ball), their momentum is going in the opposite direction that you are going. Therefore, all you need to do is move the ball out of the way of their incoming foot and push it forward with the foot that received the pass from the other foot. Being explosive after the skill helps, but not nearly as much as it does for a feint because all the defender's momentum is going in the opposite direction you are going.

. As a result, once the defender misses the ball when they have jumped in, they will have to completely come to a stop and then start sprinting at full speed again back towards the direction they came. **To go from a full sprint to a stop back to a full sprint takes a considerable amount of time.** For many players, this move is not as easy to master initially as a roll would be, however, it is much faster and more efficient of a skill when you have it mastered.

3. A "shot fake" is when you fake a shot. Similarly, you can do a pass fake when you pretend to make a pass. These are used anywhere on the field, but as you travel closer to the net, what would have typically been a pass fake, now is more

likely to be a shot fake. As you travel closer to the goal, the other team understands your objective is to shoot and to score. **Shot fakes are very helpful at making the defender flinch/freeze for half a second so that you can change your direction and explode/accelerate away with speed.** Shot fakes are great whether the defender is close to you or far away.

When the defender is several yards away from you, they will flinch because they do not want to be hit with the ball when you pretend to shoot it. If they are very close to you when you do a shot fake, they will overreach thinking that you will shoot the ball. They will try to reach out to stop the "shot," which allows you to cut the ball and change your direction while accelerating away. **To do a shot fake correctly, you must make it look exactly like a shot.** That means the shooting leg must go all the way back and your arms go up exactly the same way as if you were going to shoot the ball.

The thing that most players do not do is lift their head slightly before they do a shot fake. In most game situations, a good striker is going to make sure they know where the goalkeeper is before they shoot the ball. If the goalkeeper has poor positioning in the net, they will shoot it where the goalie is not in the net. Otherwise, when they take a quick glance at the net and see the goalie has proper positioning, a great striker will shoot where the goalie is not (often to the far post).

Shooting to the part of the net where the goalie is not located means that the striker must shoot a more tactical and challenging shot on net, in order to score. However, because you are doing a shot fake, the defender will notice if you did not lift your head for a glance. **They will realize that your shot fakes differ from your real shots and they will have more success defending against you because you did not make your shot and your shot fake look the same.**

4. A "Cut" is used to change directions. Add a shot fake to this skill and it makes for a great skill to change your direction while giving you space. **A cut is simply stopping the ball with the inside or outside of your foot and then pushing the ball in a direction that is different than the direction you were previously dribbling.** To correctly perform a cut (also known as a chop) with the outside of your foot, your leg that is cutting the ball must step entirely past the ball. Then, allow the ball to hit your foot, which effectively stops the ball.

Since the ball is on the outside of your foot, the outside of the foot cut is perfect to accelerate away because the ball is perfectly where you would need it to be to push it using your laces with your toe down and in. **An inside of the foot cut is often better used when you are along a sideline** pretending to cross the ball and you cut the ball to keep it in front of you to attack in a different direction.

Parenting Tip:

-A "scissor" is not the same thing as a step over. **A step over is when you are next to the ball and you have your furthest leg from the ball step over the ball, so your entire body turns as if you are going one way, but miss the ball so you can accelerate in the opposite direction.** A scissor is when the foot closest to the ball goes around the ball as you are attacking in a game. A step over is excellent to use along the sidelines whereas it is best to use the scissor (similar to a feint) when attacking a defender that is back pedaling/jockeying you. See the image on the next page for an example of a step over.

Coaching Tip:

-Many players train and practice the scissor. The scissor is okay at best, but it requires an extra step to plant in front of the ball. An additional step allows the player to be past the ball enough so that when you pretend to push it in one direction past the defender, the ball can roll between your legs and you can accelerate in the other direction.

Most people teach the scissor in a way that makes it look like a "magic wand." Imagine a magic show you have seen on television, in movies, or in real life where the magician waves their wand over their hat. That is what most players' scissor looks like because they throw their leg over the ball, but not actually go around the ball. Also, they never turn their hips, so the defender is infrequently faked out by the foot skill. **The scissor is okay to practice if you have the body feint down perfectly, but the feint is more efficient than the scissor.**

Chapter 6

Dribbling

The ability to dribble a ball is essential to be productive on the field. There are several points to consider in order to dribble correctly that will ensure your success on the soccer field and are as follows:

1. Keep the toe of your dribbling foot down and in
2. Less touches will allow you to dribble faster
3. Use less touches when you have more space
4. Raise your head slightly
5. Practice dribbling with both feet

1. **You want your toe down and in on the foot that is pushing the ball, which places you on the balls of your feet.** See the "A" in the picture on the previous page for where the balls of your feet are located. When a coach tells you to run on your toes, they are really saying to run on the toes and the balls of your feet. Therefore, anytime you go on your "tippy-toes," you are really on your toes and the balls of your feet. Having your toes "down and in" on the foot you are pushing the ball with makes a cupping shape (think of a shape similar to an ice cream scooper) with your foot that allows the ball to fit perfectly on your laces as you push the ball with each step. Notice that it is "toe down and in." You must turn it slightly inside so that you can effectively push the ball with your laces. Otherwise, you will be poking it forward and you are not going to be able to run with much speed if your toe is just down. You will end up hitting the ground way too often with your toes, which will slow you down.

2. Something that dramatically changed my speed of play overnight was that **the more space you have, the fewer touches you want to take as a soccer player**. The more touches you take, the more time it takes to travel the same amount of distance. Taking unnecessary touches allows the defender more time to close you down, steal the ball, or for players on the opposing team to hustle back to provide support in stopping you. This concept is counter-intuitive for most players as they think more touches means more skill, which will result in them being a better soccer player. In fact, in a recent college soccer player training class I was conducting, I noticed that many of the college players took two or three more touches to cover space that could have easily been done in one touch.

3. The closer the person defending is to you, the smaller the touches you will want to take, except when you take your explosive touch after a skill to push away from the defender. **Also, if you are dribbling in a congested portion of the field, such as the central midfield area, you will generally take smaller touches.** The center midfielders have defenders, outside midfielder, and forwards creeping into their space. Let us not forget they also likely have another center midfielder on their team and two from the opposing team to consider in their area too.

In these instances, because there are so many people around a center midfielder, they generally will and should take smaller touches than an outside midfielder, forward, or outside defender. Smaller touches will allow a center midfielder to be in closer contact with the ball. Therefore, they can quickly push and dribble the ball away from an opposing team player's foot. **However, as a forward with more space and especially an outside midfielder who has a ton of room on the soccer field, taking bigger touches allows you to have an explosive attack and a very good counterattack when your team steals possession of the ball.**

4. **An important point to keep in mind when dribbling is that you want your head raised a bit so that you are looking about 5 yards in front of you while you dribble.** Looking ahead of you makes it so you can still see the ball in your peripheral vision, but you can also now see the defenders and other teammates' positioning on the field. Being a good dribbler is as much about being able to take good touches as it is being able to pick your head up to see if there is a better option on the field for you than for you to keep dribbling.

Let us face it, we have all played with that person that is exceptionally good at dribbling and quite entertaining to watch, but who keeps their head down the entire time when they dribble. Though they may be doing some productive things with the ball, they are not doing nearly as many constructive actions as a player who picks their head up a little bit. The other team is going to recognize that the person keeps their head down while they dribble and so they will apply more pressure to them and lessen pressure on other players because they realize he or she does not look up to know where their teammates are located on the field. **Lastly, they are not very fun to play with because they hardly pass the ball to anyone.**

5. Naturally, being able to dribble with both feet is very important. **In fact, being a better dribbler with your opposite foot than with your dominant foot will make you a better soccer player.** Many of the skills you use to beat a defender will make it so that you fake to take it with your opposite foot, but then you can push and take it with your strong foot to either continue dribbling or to take a shot. Having a strong opposite foot was something I did not realize was necessary for the longest time. I would do a lot of dribbling with my dominant right foot, which would then (after I did a skill) put me on my left foot for a shot. In fact, I have compensated so much for it that I probably take twice as many shots with my opposite foot as I do with my dominant foot. Had I developed a stronger opposite foot, it would have resulted in more shots with my dominant foot.

Keep in mind that in most game situations, a good defender is going to push you to your opposite foot. As a result, I score more goals with my left foot since I take more shots with my left foot because I am a slightly better dribbler with my right foot. Avoid this as much as possible and learn to be a good dribbler with your opposite foot so after a skill, the ball will be on your dominant foot when you go to shoot. After all, dribbling is what you do to place the ball where you want it, whether you will be looking to shoot the ball or make a pass. If you cannot dribble well, you are not going to have many opportunities to pass the ball and you will not have many opportunities to shoot the ball. Learn which skills are most important to know in the third book in the series – *Soccer Dribbling & Foot Skills: A Step-by-Step Guide on How to Dribble Past the Other Team.*

Parenting Tip:

-When dribbling, slowing yourself down reduces your momentum tremendously. Slowing down decreases your ability to make progress on the field, which makes it very easy for the other team to catch up with you. Ideally, when dribbling, remain at as high of a speed as possible to avoid more of the opposing team's defenders and midfielders hustling back to provide support and take the ball. However, please keep in mind that running faster while you dribble will slightly increase your chances of making a mistake. Avoiding mistakes at your top speed is one of the many reasons why it is so important to practice at game speed.

Coaching Tip:

-An excellent way to start a practice is with fast footwork to work on dribbling. Yes, even for high school and college-level players, focusing on making sure that they are taking a touch with their toe down and in and having their head raised is more important than many of the skills that can be used while you dribble. When you practice dribbling, vary it between speed dribbling and taking small touches. **Speed dribbling is when you take a touch every single step, but your step is a very long stride.** Also, include small touch dribbling to develop their habit of having their toe down and in. It allows you to take a lot more touches in the same amount of space because you are not using as long of a stride. When practicing taking small touches, you are really going for a large quantity of touches.

Chapter 7

Defending

As a defender, you want your body positioning to be angled. You never want to completely have your hips pointed ("squared") at the attacker because then it makes it so that the attacker can go to the right of you, to the left of you, and between your legs. **You want to be angled, but not entirely turned to the side.** Position one of your sides so it is facing the attacker, but still at a diagonal. If it were hands on a clock, you would want your feet positioning just like the hands on the clock at either "10 and 4," as shown in the first image or "8 and 2," as shown in the second image.

This body positioning will allow you to push them either to the left or the right. Standing at "10 and 4" would push them to their left foot and standing at "8 and 2" would push them to their right foot. Keep in mind that just standing directly in front of them and turning your hips will not force them in the direction that you want them to go. **You must be slightly off-centered with your hips set at either "10 and 4" or "8 and 2," to push them in the direction that you want them to go.** If you just turn your hips directly in front of a good dribbler, they will attack the side that you are not facing, all other things being equal, to make it easier for themselves.

As a defender, it is essential that you are actively on your toes. You do not want to be standing still. You want to be bent at the knees, bent at the hips, and lower in your stance. This will allow you to accelerate faster when the attacker does a skill and tries to sprint away. One thing that nearly all trainees do not realize is that they need to make themselves bigger.

The most straightforward and easiest way to do that is to pick your arms up. **In a game, 19 out of 20 times, the referee is not going to call you if your arms are up.** From a young age, they teach you that you must keep your arms by your side. However, if the referee is not going to be calling your arms being up in a game, then you should not worry about keeping your arms down. Extend your elbow and your shoulder to engage with them. It is crucial that you make yourself look bigger than you are for a few reasons:

-An attacker seeing you as being bigger will naturally cause their confidence to decrease.

-It makes it a little bit harder for them to travel around you because you can use your arm to generate momentum as you turn, which will turn your waist/hips more quickly than if you were just turning without the use of your arms.

-Having your arms up will make it easier for you to place your forearm against their bodies and use your shoulder muscle to keep them away from the ball. If you ever watch professional defenders, they tend to use their hands and arms a lot because, in most situations, the referee is not going to call anything against them.

Parenting Tip:

-In a 1v1 game situation, where you push the defender depends on the portion of the field they are on and their location relative to your teammates. Ideally, if you are in the middle of the field, you would want to push the attacker to their weak foot. How do you know which foot is there weak foot? **Always assume it is their left foot until they prove you otherwise.** However, when you are along a sideline and it is still a one versus one, you want to position your body in a way that will push them towards the sideline and out of bounds.

Coaching Tip:

-If you have another defender supporting you, a good attacker is going to take a route that requires them to beat only one defender. However, **a good defender is going to push the attacker into their partner** to increase the probability that they can take the ball away because two players' feet reaching at the ball will likely be a lot better than one player's feet reaching to take the ball.

Chapter 8

Passing the Ball

As a soccer player, it is important to have the fundamentals down when it comes to passing. You can pass the ball with different parts of your foot, but the form that should be your most frequently used passing form is with the inside of your foot as follows:

1. Plant next to the ball while pointing your foot and hips at your partner
2. Toe up, heel down, and ankle locked
3. Knees slightly bent and foot slightly off the ground
4. Follow through after making contact with the ball

1. The form for a pass and shot are different. **With passing form, you can (and should) plant much closer to the ball because your body mechanics allow you to turn your leg and pass the ball with the inside of your foot.** Similarly to a shot, you want to have the leg that is planting on the ground pointed at the person or the open space to which you are passing the ball. You have your plant leg slightly bent, which is the same for your shooting form. You definitely do not want a straight leg when you will plant for a shot or a pass. Also, turn your hips towards the person or area on the field that you are passing the ball.

2. **Point your toe all the way up, which makes your heel go down.** Having your toe up and heal down naturally locks your ankle. Having a locked ankle will make it so that you have a powerful and more accurate pass. Also, locking your ankle allows the surface of your foot that you are passing the ball with (the side of your foot) to be wider. A wider foot creates less room for error so that if you miscalculate a little bit where the ball will be, you have a broader surface to ensure a more accurate pass. Conversely, if your toe is pointed down and your heel is up, your ankle will be loose, resulting in a lack of power on your pass. Also, you are making your foot smaller and narrower, which means that your pass will be inaccurate if misjudged even slightly for where the ball will be.

3. **Have the knee from your passing leg slightly bent.** You do not want a straight leg when you are passing. In fact, you do not want straight legs in nearly all game instances. When you straighten your leg and you stand completely up it makes it so that you are not engaging the strongest muscle group of your legs, which is the quadriceps. It makes it so that you are not going to be as explosive with your shooting, passing, dribbling, running, jumping, etc. Having a bent leg naturally makes it so that your foot will be slightly off the ground. If you pass the ball with your foot touching the ground or close to the ground, the pass will result in the ball popping up in the air. Part of passing is to make sure that you are making it as easy as possible for your teammate. After all, soccer is a team sport, so if you are consistently passing the ball in the air, you are making it more difficult for your teammates. Your teammates will likely then have to focus their first touch on trapping the ball on the ground and then their second touch of the ball allows them to attack in the space. Ideally, your pass is firm, accurate, and on the ground so that their first touch can be into space on the field.

4. **Next, make sure you follow through on your pass.** What you do with your leg after you fully follow through depends on the situation that you are in during the game, scrimmage, or practice. Most times, after you make a pass, you will be running to another spot on the field to keep developing the play. Therefore, as you pass the ball (similar

to a shot), you follow through and land on your passing foot. Then, you bring your back leg forward to take the next step. As you pass, you are already starting to continue to run and maintain your forward motion to the next spot on the field that you want to go. However, at times you will be passing the ball and you are not going to be a part of the attacking portion of that play. For example, players that may do this are a goalie or in a few instances, a defender. Therefore, you follow through after you pass the ball, but then you bring your leg back to where it began the passing motion. As a result, you end up in the same spot you started when you are making this pass.

Parenting Tip:

-Keeping your head down while you pass the ball keeps your chest over the ball and holds your form together for a more accurate pass. **Having your head over the ball reduces the chance that the ball will pop up into the air when you pass the ball.**

Coaching Tip:

-Keep most of your passes on the ground when playing to a teammate. However, if you are playing on a field of low quality that is bumpy in certain places, then consider passing slightly off the ground. If you pass on the ground, it increases your chance of hitting a bumpy spot on the field, which will pop the ball into the air and slow its forward progress. By putting the ball in the air, slightly off the ground, it reduces the chance of it hitting a rough spot and increases the probability that it is a good pass. Furthermore, pass the ball to a position that helps your teammate. **Generally, lead your teammate with a pass when there is no one in front of them.** In most circumstances, avoid passing behind your teammate because they must come to a complete stop and turn around to receive the pass if they were running up the field. However, this is appropriate when you are a defender passing to another defender on your team that has someone covering them.

Chapter 9

Receiving the Ball

You can receive the ball with different parts of your foot, but the five general rules to receive a pass, listed in chronological order to ensure ball control and an accurate first touch are:

1. Plant next to the ball while pointing your foot and hips at your teammate
2. Toe up, heel down, and ankle locked
3. Knees slightly bent
4. Foot slightly off the ground
5. Typically, use the inside of the foot towards the heel to take an attacking touch

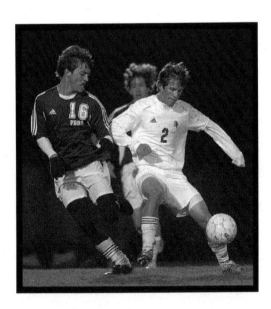

The form to receive a pass is the same as the first four steps of the form to make a pass. However, to receive a pass, there are a few more things to consider to make sure that you are productive with the ball:

1. **Demand the ball; do not ask for the ball. Yell for the ball; do not call for the ball.** These shifts in wording (demand versus ask and yell versus call) do a few excellent things for you as the person that wants to receive a pass or be played a through ball. A through ball is when someone plays the ball in front of you and into space allowing you to run to the ball and continue your forward momentum at full speed.

Demanding the ball lets the person that is passing the ball know that you are very confident. It tells him or her that you will do something with the ball that is beneficial for your team. Think about it, if you are playing a game and have two people that you can pass the ball. The first person is screaming their head off demanding the ball. The other person is maybe showing for a pass, using a hand motion indicating that they want the ball, or meekly asking for the ball. Even if the person that is yelling for the ball is not quite as open, the player with the ball will consider passing it to them because they can hear it in their voice that they plan to do something with the ball. Also, demanding/yelling for the ball even if the person with the ball is close to you, ensures that he or she hears you.

Often, the person dribbling the ball is far away from you or potentially has a defender or two covering them. Therefore, by demanding/yelling for the ball, you let them know that you are open to receive the ball. **Many available passes in soccer are not made because the player with the ball did not know you were open.** They have their head down and looking at the ball, to protect the ball from the defender. Therefore, if they do not hear you with their ears, they are likely not going to see you with their eyes. Lastly, yelling for the ball builds confidence in yourself and increases your ability to help your team achieve its offensive objective of scoring!

2. **Depending on the situation in the game, you want to make sure that you check to the ball (go towards the ball) in most instances.** Now, you definitely do not want to do that when you are making a "through" run and you want them to play the pass in front of you. In these situations, you want to communicate (yell/hand motion/or start sprinting in a direction away from the play, but down the field) to them where you are going and let them pass the ball in front of you so that you can take your first touch in stride. More often than not, you will be receiving a pass and you should be checking to the ball to make sure that you successfully receive the ball.

One of the more frustrating things for a coach and a teammate is when you are passed a good (not a great) pass and you are not able to receive the ball because you are playing lazily. You must be active, on your toes, and going to receive the pass. If you do not, it allows the defender to come between you and the ball. This laziness results in an intercepted pass, which makes it very easy for the other team to have a counterattack due to you losing possession during a simple pass.

3. **Before receiving a pass, make sure to scan the field and look behind you.** Having a good idea of what you plan to do before you actually do it will make you a much more effective and efficient soccer player, as well as a better teammate. It does not have to be a 5 to 10-second scan. It is just a quick swivel of the head to see if there is pressure and where some open teammates are for you to make a sensible pass or potentially dribble after you receive the ball. A quick look is something that sets college players apart from high school players and definitely professional players from college players.

These differences are things that coaches and scouts notice. An excellent defender, midfielder, or striker will assuredly know where teammates and opponents are on the field. Therefore, as they are receiving the pass, they are already thinking about what their next actions in the game will be. In soccer and life, if you fail to plan, you plan to fail. **By quickly scanning behind you, you are already starting to allow yourself mentally to have time to develop a plan of attack.** The fast scan will surely help you score more or deliver the pass that will allow your team to score.

4. **Next, when you receive a pass in most game situations, you still want your hips to be square with your teammate.** Though when you are along a sideline this advice may change, being squared with your teammate means that you are pointing your hips at your teammate. When your hips are square with your teammate, you will be more accurate with your first touch than if your hips are not pointing at your teammate. In this instance, you are creating an L with your stance by pointing your plant foot at your teammate. The foot you are receiving the pass with is turned, so that you can use the inside of your foot to take your first touch. This form is basically the same as if you were making a pass.

5. **Roughly 95% of your first touches in a game should be attacking touches.** An attacking touch pushes the ball into space with your first touch. An attacking touch is the opposite of taking a touch where the ball stops underneath you (at your feet). An attacking touch may go towards your opponents net, towards your own net, or in any direction away from where you are currently. In a game, you should mostly be taking attacking touches because it allows you,

with your first touch, to already have the ball going in the direction that you want to take it.

More often than not, the first attacking touch is into space on the field to give yourself more time to think, to pass, to dribble, to shoot, to do whatever you need to do with the ball. Next, by taking the first step with your attacking touch, you will have a more accurate first touch. Looking at the picture, use part "B" to take an attacking touch with the hardest part of your foot, which can be referred to as the "bat."

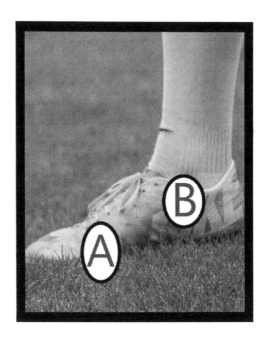

Your attacking touch is not meant to push the ball really far away from you; it is intended for you to take your first step in the direction that you want to go. **An attacking**

touch was something I did not realize for the longest time that was key to being a fast soccer player. I thought that you had to be a quick runner to be a fast soccer player. In reality, you have to be great with your first attacking touch to be a fast soccer player. This one tip alone changed my game overnight. The attacking touch helps your acceleration tremendously because you are already starting to build momentum and speed in the direction that you want to go, which enables you to distance yourself from the defender that is marking you.

6. **Occasionally, it will be appropriate to take a touch underneath your body (a touch that stops at your feet).** This touch is necessary when you have too many people around you where someone could easily cut an attacking touch off and take possession of the ball from you. Only then is it okay to take your first touch under your body. Also, if you receive a difficult pass, ideally you still take an attacking first touch, but it is understandable if you take a first touch that stops underneath you and then you start attacking with the ball. Bad passes are generally ones played to you in the air. Looking at the picture again, use part "A" to take a touch with the softest portion of your foot, which can be referred to as the "broom" to settle the ball at your feet.

7. When you move to receive the pass, what you plan to do with the ball determines which portion of your foot to use to take an attacking touch. **Ideally, the attacking touch is**

really going to be an attacking step. You are pushing the ball with the same portion of your foot (the inside of your ankle) that you pass a ball with because it should be locked and will push the ball better. However, if you are looking for the ball to stop underneath you, you will be taking your first touch with the inside of your foot up towards your toes.

There is space in your shoe between your toes, there is a lot more fabric, and a lot less bone towards your toes. This area of your foot is your "broom" and because your "broom" is not very hard, the ball will stop underneath you. Look at the portion of the foot labeled "A" in the previous image. Additionally, if you are looking to have your first touch go completely behind you so that you can continue to accelerate away from pressure and into space, then you can take the touch even more softly towards the inside of your foot using your toes (using the "broom"). Do this more softly than if you wanted to stop the ball underneath you. This much softer touch is so that the ball does not go racing by you. You can slow it down a little bit, but not stop it entirely because you want to be attacking in the space directly behind you.

Parenting Tip:

-**Use the inside of your right foot to take an attacking touch to the right and use the inside of your left foot to take an attacking touch to the left.** Using the correct foot will make it so that you do not cross your feet, which is incredibly unathletic. Also, you will have more accurate attacking touches when you do not cross your feet.

Coaching Tip:

-**In practice, require that your team demands/yells for the ball at all times.** Whether it is in a drill and you know exactly where the pass is coming from or not, prepare yourself and have your team establishing the habit of always demanding and yelling for the ball. By using mental energy to create habits in practice, you will not have to focus on it in a game. Creating habits is precisely one of the critical points of practicing - you create the habits to use in a game. After all, it has been said that perfect practice makes perfect, so expect nothing less than perfection from your team in practices.

Chapter 10

Weight Training

As an athlete, you are looking to give yourself any ethically possible edge that you can. Whether it is your mindset, knowledge about how to score, how to defend, how to be faster, how to be more explosive, how to be stronger, how to be more difficult to push off the ball, etc. **Weight training is critical for an athlete to develop excellent abilities off the field that will be applicable on the field.** It is essential to try to emphasize moves that are as beneficial as possible but do not consume an excessive amount of time, energy, or emotional capital, which, in the short-term, would take away from training for the game you love. What this means is biceps curls and triceps extensions are not going to make a meaningful difference in your playing career. However, your ability to perform the big three compound lifts will.

The big three are squatting, deadlifting, and bench pressing. Furthermore, since this sport is all about having strong legs, doing some leg presses, calf raises, and lunges will also be very beneficial. You are in a sport that is one of the most calorie consuming competitions around. Due to all the running, you will expend a lot of calories. Therefore, unless you are a larger soccer player looking to lose weight, spending hours and hours in the weight room is not going to be beneficial for you. However, emphasizing a few key weightlifting moves will be very helpful even though they do not take that much time to do.

If you have access to a weight room or gym, the moves to emphasize and to perfect are the **squat** (where the bar is on your back you are squatting and then standing back up using your hips, quadriceps, hamstrings, and glutes to name a few of the muscles). This lift is known as the king of mass building for a reason. It is a move that should be a part of all the weight trainers lifting routines, granted there are no previous injuries that prevent the athlete from doing any variation of the squat. Different variations of the squat are the back squat, front squat, sumo squat, bodyweight/air squat, machine squat, hack squat, kettlebell/goblet squat, Smith

Machine squat, Zercher squat, and box squat. If you have previous injuries that prevent certain ranges of motion, try all the variations and select the one that you can use the most weight on that works your muscles and does not cause pain to your joints, ligaments, and tendons.

Next, the **deadlift** is to build overall power. This move is when a bar filled with weight is on the ground, you bend down (emphasizing your leg muscles), and you pick up the weight while making sure to drive your hips forward. You are likely noticing the common theme in these first two lifts is the ability to have your hips working. As an athlete, having strong hips will make you a faster runner, give you strength to make it harder for you to be pushed off of the ball, make you much more explosive as you start to sprint and it will allow you to have more powerful shots.

Additionally, though the **bench press** is not specifically for the lower body, it will help develop your upper body and it will help build confidence. As you begin to gain muscle in your chest, shoulders, and triceps from practicing this move, your self-esteem will soar. A bench press is when you lie with your back on a bench and you press the bar away from your body.

Also, include **pull-ups** as these are a great exercise to develop your back muscles. These can be done in many places as long as there is a bar, or a tree branch, or a rail... Whether your grip is a reverse grip (also known as a chin-up), neutral grip, narrow grip, standard grip, or wide grip, pull-ups strengthen your back muscles and depending on your hand grips, pull-ups can build your forearms and biceps too, based on the variation of pull-up that you perform.

Next, if you have a gym, **leg presses** are great for adding on leg mass and gaining leg power. It entails sitting in the machine and using your leg muscles to push the platform. Leg pressing increases your speed, how high you can jump, and how hard you can kick a ball.

Furthermore, **calf raises** are when you push your entire body further up in the air by moving your ankle and pressing the floor down with the balls of your feet. You can perform calf raises on the leg press platform, with dumbbells in your hands, or with a barbell along your back. It will help you to be more explosive, change direction more quickly, run faster, as well as allowing your body to react more rapidly to the ball.

When you are in the gym, you will want to emphasize rep ranges of no more than 6 to 8 reps to develop strength applicable to the field, without packing on muscle that does not help you in the sport you love. Higher rep ranges of 20+ reps will help with your endurance, but what you should be looking for in the gym is gaining more strength. **Emphasizing strength is best accomplished by performing a set of 6 repetitions or less to failure.** Failing within the 8 to 12 rep range is going to make it so that you are seeking muscular size (hypertrophy). Training for muscular size is not wrong because it will lead to some strength gains and more endurance, but it does not directly line up with becoming better as an athlete if that is your overarching goal.

If you do not have access to a gym, some good exercises to perform are squats, lunges, sit-ups, leg raises, planks, push-ups, and supermans. Let us say you are just on the soccer field and it is only you. Squatting or jump squatting will be great for developing leg strength and explosiveness.

Next, **lunging** is where you extend one leg in front of your body and one leg behind your body and you go down in what you would think would look like a half squat with just one leg. Lunging is an exercise that you want to make sure you do as many reps with the right leg as you do with the left. Similarly to squats, you can perform lunges with jumps if they are too easy to do without any additional weight. Also, putting your back foot up on something, like the first row of the bleachers or a chair it becomes what is known as a Bulgarian squat. Lifting up your leg will give you a little bit of variation in your lunge and because your leg is up on something, it will make the lunge a little bit more difficult.

Sit-ups are when your upper body hinges up at the waist as you lie on your back. You use your abs (abdominals) to raise your upper body up. Also, perform leg raises where instead of bringing your upper body up, you bring your legs up. Too many people emphasize sit-ups over leg raises because for leg raises, you have to raise up your legs, which weigh more than your upper body does. Therefore, doing leg raises is going to help you obtain six pack abs a lot quicker than doing sit-ups or crunches will. However, both are important because the sit-ups and crunches emphasize your upper abs whereas the leg raises accentuate the lower abs.

Furthermore, **planks** are where you either have your arms extended straight out (at the top of push-up position) or where you have your forearms and elbows on the ground, while your body is straight as well. A plank works your transverse abdominis, which allows you to work the layer of muscle underneath the ab muscles that you would see if you had six pack abs. Planks help you push out your abs, so they become more visible. Developing spectacular abs gives you more confidence, assists in stabilizing your body, and makes you a better athlete.

Push-ups are great to do and similarly to bench pressing, they will develop your pecs (chest), deltoids (shoulders), and triceps (the back of your arms). Though gaining upper body mass is not paramount for this sport, it does boost confidence and increase overall strength. Also, it does not take much additional time to perform a few extra sets on the field after you have done your leg day exercises.

Supermans are an exercise where you lie prone on your stomach. Extend your legs behind you and raise your arms into the air. These are good at developing your glutes, your lower back, shoulders, and your trapezius.

If you do not have a gym where you can add additional weights, and you are just doing these exercises out on the soccer field, doing higher repetitions to failure is going to be much better than not doing it at all or stopping short of failure. It is okay if you are doing push-ups into the 30s or 40s, sit-ups into the 60s or 80s, and many jump squats. Make sure with every exercise that you focus on good form. Weight training is crucial for building confidence. As you gain strength, you will become more confident on the field.

As you exercise and lift more, granted that you are consuming more calories, you will start to gain muscle. As you grow muscle, this will also help you boost your confidence because you will begin to feel more comfortable and have higher self-esteem about your body. Yes, the strength and size take time, but greatness takes time and even just by you reading this book, you are showing that there is greatness in you that wants to come out.

Parenting Tip:

-**Always emphasize good form.** Similarly to completing a drill, you do not want any exercises to be sloppy. Poor form push-ups, really quick crunches where you can see they are just hurting their neck and back more than it is developing their abs, or squats where they only go a quarter of the way down and are putting all of their body weight into their knees will inevitably lead to injuries. Be a stickler for quality over quantity and quality over the amount of time it takes when doing any exercises.

Coaching Tip:

-Developing the abilities that you utilize in a game is most important to do in practices. Performing passing, dribbling, and attacking drills are more important than focusing on weight training or calisthenics (bodyweight exercises). However, consider ending a practice with some sprints, squat jumps, split-legged jump lunges, push-ups, sit-ups, leg raises, supermans, planks, or some long jumps. **Perform the exercises at the end of your practice because you do not want to tire your players before you even start training since it increases the chance of injury.**

Chapter 11

Nutrition

As you read this chapter, please keep in mind that I am not a certified dietitian, a certified trainer, or a medical practitioner. However, I am a person with tens of thousands of hours of experience on the field, in the weight room, and in the kitchen. Currently, I have read well over 250 nutrition, fitness, bodybuilding, and health magazines, in addition to over 40 nutrition, food science, and weight-training books. Having placed the insights into practice, I have realized that there is much more to be learned in the execution than there is only in the reading/listening about a subject.

This book provides the understanding, but the application of the concepts offers the in-depth knowledge. You can understand a lot from reading, but applying what you read is how you take yourself from a novice level to an amateur level, an amateur level to a proficient level, or from a proficient level to a professional level. I started out as a chubby child, went to the point of being too skinny because I did not eat enough food, and now I have finally found the sweet spot. I have maintained 8-pack abs for over a decade and definitely the look of a fit athlete. I state these facts about myself not to brag or impress you, but to express that having a good nutrition plan is critical for being healthy, looking the way you want to look, and increasing your performance on the field. With that in mind, countless hours of experimenting, trials, and errors have occurred to develop what works best for a soccer player.

Nutrient timing is critical to an athlete. You do not want to go into a game after drinking half a gallon of milk and eating an entire tub of cottage cheese. You will feel slow, your legs will feel heavier, and you will not perform very well. Also, it is not advisable to go to bed after eating half a loaf of bread and drinking two bottles of soda pop because all of the carbohydrates will spike your blood sugar and energy levels. The bread and soda will likely keep you awake from the spike in blood sugar and much of that meal will not be used to provide energy. If it is not used to produce energy, it will likely be stored as fat. Also, the caffeine from the soda pop will keep you restless.

One of the most important things for an athlete is having a minimum of 7 quality hours of sleep per night. Before bed, you want a slower digesting meal, so foods that are high in fiber, high in fat, and high in protein. Some things to consider consuming are nuts, seeds, meat, different kinds of nut butter (almond, cashew, and to a lesser extent, peanut butter). Upon awakening in the morning, your body has likely used up most of its glycogen (blood sugar) stores throughout the night, so consume foods that are higher in carbohydrates. Examples are fruits, vegetables, and healthy grains such as quinoa, brown rice, sweet potatoes, steel-cut oatmeal, and organic bread (though there are mixed reviews on bread given that it has gluten).

These carbohydrates are very beneficial to replenish your glycogen stores and gives you the energy to help you function appropriately until your next meal. Furthermore, there is a common practice in the athletic world that you are supposed to "carb up" the night before a game. Say you have an upcoming game and consume a pasta dinner the night before, to obtain sufficient carbohydrates in your system. However, in reality, you want to eat some carbohydrates, but do not need to eat three bowls of pasta the night before a game.

It will be more beneficial for you to consume carbs closer to the event, but this depends on how well your body digests food and how empty or full you prefer to be starting a game. Often, 2 to 4 hours before a match is an ideal time to take in more carbohydrates in the form of faster-digesting vegetables, such as carrots and fruits such as apples, bananas, or watermelon, as well as carbohydrates such as quinoa, sweet potatoes or brown rice. If carbs will be consumed immediately before a game, then use faster-digesting carbs such as white potatoes.

After a game and after exercise, it is ideal to take in nutrition to help build your muscle fibers. You break your muscles down anytime you use them. When they are provided enough quality nutrition and rest, they will grow back stronger. Therefore, when you go to do the same activity, you will be able to perform better, quicker, and more efficiently.

Things that would be good to consume after a physical performance would be foods that are high in carbohydrates and fast-digesting protein. An example that is easy to obtain is organic milk. Though the evidence shows altering views on lactose, having some organic milk after a workout or a whey protein shake with non-GMO dextrose is beneficial. **You want to take in enough carbohydrates to spike up your blood sugar a little bit after a game or workout so that it helps utilize the protein that you will be taking in.**

Whey protein is one of the most bio-available and quickest digesting proteins that you can use that is great before and after a workout. If you will be drinking milk, it has milk protein, which is 20% whey protein and 80% casein protein. It is essential that if after a workout you have more physical activities later in the day, you take in enough carbohydrates to replenish your glycogen. It is critical to minimize the amount of fat and fiber that you will be taking in the post-workout 30-minute window after a workout because fiber and fat are slower digesting. They slow the absorption of vitamins, minerals, and nutrients. Avoid very dense foods like spinach or peanut butter unless there is absolutely nothing else that you can consume. Something healthy is better than nothing.

When it comes to nutrition, you have likely heard it before a hundred times that "you are what you eat." Something that you may have never heard or read is that **you are what your food eats** too. Therefore, it is vital that you have high-quality food. If the cow, chicken, pig, turkey, or fish that you are eating is consuming nutritious food too, those animals will provide more value than other poorly fed animals.

Having food that you know is eating other living organisms and healthy food, you will have much more vitamin-rich, nutrient-dense, mineral-packed food. Healthy food is in direct opposition to the salmon that is farm-raised eating soy pellets, the chicken that is caged, and the cow that is eating a mix of canola meal and cottonseed hulls. These types of animal meats provide lackluster nutrition that will give you the same amount of protein, fat, and carbohydrates. However, concerning the higher levels of nutrition (the vitamins, minerals, nutrients, antioxidants, phytonutrients, and even more things about food that have not been discovered yet) they will be lacking.

Not all vegetables are created equal. Though plants do not eat other food, they do absorb nutrients from the soil, and if you consume genetically modified food, they too will be lacking in the rich nutrients that is a must for your fruits, vegetables, and grains. The most genetically modified foods on the market are sugar, canola, cottonseed, soy, squash, zucchini, alfalfa, and corn. These are foods that scientists have gone into and changed the structure of the organism. Frequently, the modification is to withstand harmful weed killers, such as glyphosate.

Many countries around the world have already banned glyphosate, but at the time of writing this book, it is still not banned in the United States of America. It helps to kill weeds that are competing for the same nutrition in the soil as the cultivated crop. **Though having fewer weeds is good in theory, using harmful and synthetic weed killers to do so is not good.** The glyphosate acts as a mineral chelator making it so that the plant does not take the nutrients, vitamins, and minerals from the soil at the rate that it would have if the soil had not been sprayed with that mineral chelator. Therefore, you will have the same amount of protein, fat, and carbohydrates from a genetically modified ear of corn versus a non-genetically modified ear of corn, however, the genetically modified corn is going to have a lot less nutritional value that is very important for an athlete.

Parenting Tip:

-Players need sleep of 7 hours at a minimum and 9 hours at a maximum. **Countless studies have shown that more or less than that range can lead to lack of motivation, lack of time, energy, and awareness.** Ensure that it is good quality sleep, so turn off any additional lights in the room and anything making noises. Similar to having your child say quality affirmations as a soccer player, you want to make sure they are telling themselves that they are a good sleeper to improve the quality and the quantity of sleep that your child can achieve. This will likely start with you. If you say how bad of a sleeper you are, your child will likely adopt your mindset and consider themselves bad sleepers too.

Coaching Tip:

-For any tournaments or days with long practices, make sure that you bring enough carbohydrates. Grab several bananas, a bag of apples, or other fruits. **Make sure at the very least your team is going to be replenishing their glycogen levels to ensure they have stored energy to use to perform in the next game.** Additionally, having a gallon of milk on ice and a few Dixie cups with you to pour some post-game nutrition (after the last game of the day) will definitely make a difference in the long-term recovery and performance of your team.

Chapter 12

Stretching/Yoga

Flexibility is significant for longevity in any athletic endeavor. However, the type of stretching or yoga moves that you want to do depend on the kind of exercise you will be doing or have already completed. **Before strenuous training, you want to engage in dynamic/ballistic stretching.** Dynamic/ballistic stretching is not where you are holding a stretch and trying to go deeper into the position for a minute or two at a time. It is where you are shaking your muscles out, performing jumping jacks, doing standing mountain climbers, and different movements to push the synovial fluid into your joints and to have the blood flowing to your muscles.

The objective is to have your muscles ready to engage in physical activity. **It is crucial that you do not hold any stretches/poses for anything more than a few seconds because it will decrease power output by up to 10% during your athletic performance.** Therefore, you would be spending time before an athletic event to reduce your performance by holding long/static stretches before you exercise. Other high-quality movements that are perfect (given no previous injuries) before physical activity are mild jogging that speeds up to fast jogging that then becomes sprinting as your body starts to become warmed up.

Furthermore, focusing on jumping and the progression of passing a ball, then softly shooting a shot, and then striking the ball with full power is excellent for warming up before a game too. Any warm-up you do, you want to start with the easiest form of that movement and then build your way up to the harder versions, the more game-like versions. You never want to start with sprinting for the beginning of your warm-up. It is better to have a nice and easy walk that turns into a jog that then becomes a few sprints.

After a game or after an athletic performance is an appropriate time to do static stretches. Your body is fatigued and very warm because you were just playing your sport and your body is very supple/flexible. Therefore, you want to work on your flexibility at that time. You are not worried about power output anymore because you have already completed your game or practice. Now, it is time to focus on being able to go deep in the stretches that will improve the longevity of your joints, as well as increase your muscle length to allow you to feel better, to recover faster, and to play the sport you love for longer.

Most athletes, especially early in their career, tend to avoid stretching because it just really does not seem like it contributes that much. This mindset and lack of action is a very nearsighted way to look at your overall game. It is not necessary to spend 30 minutes warming up before a game and another 30 minutes cooling down after a game. **However, it is suggested that you take 5-10 minutes before you will start striking a ball or begin playing in a game.**

Cool down after a game. Pick a few basic stretches to perform for your hamstrings, quadriceps, glutes, hip flexors, adductors, abductors, and calves. Have one exercise or one stretch for each one of those muscles at a minimum, which you perform after your athletic performance and have it as a routine/habit that you do after every single game. After the first few times you stretch, you will not even have to think about it anymore. A consistent theme throughout this entire book is to create the habit of the important things so that the habit can create the future you. It will take some mental effort to establish these. However, once you set them up, they become natural, and you almost feel like something is missing when you do not do them. Frequently, you go on autopilot to where you are not even aware that you are doing them until you are more than halfway through the stretches.

Similarly, before you play a game or have a practice, you also want to perform the dynamic/ballistic stretching before any weight training. You should never start with your maximum bench press weight on the bar. You want to start with just the bar and then add weight to each side and increasingly do that until your body, your joints, and your muscles feel ready to engage fully in that exercise. **The few minutes to warm up before exercising and cooling down after physical activity are steps to make sure that your body stays fit and healthy.** If you go onto the field, you should choose to warm up before you play and you are not truly done until after you cool down after the athletic game. Include a cool-down jog and the static stretches to make sure that you are improving flexibility to reduce the chance of injury before moving on to your next thing that day.

Parenting Tip:

-With one or both arms, while standing, pulling one foot behind your body (to where you are bending at the knee) will stretch your quadriceps (the muscle along the front of your thighs). While standing, putting one ankle over the other leg's knee and push on the knee of the stretching leg to stretch your gluteus (your butt) and your abductors (the muscle along the outside of your thigh). Having both feet on the ground and reaching down (bending to touch your toes) will stretch your hamstrings (the muscle along the back of your thighs).

Sitting on the ground and pulling your ankles in between your legs, while bending at the knees and pushing your elbows into your knees will stretch your adductors (the muscle along the inside of your thigh). Go into a lunge and put the back leg's knee on the ground while driving your hips towards the floor. Using your arms to push against the knee in front of you, push your upper body backward to stretch out your hip flexor (the muscle atop the front of your thigh, where your hip is). In plank position, drive your hips back (go into downward dog, but only be on the balls of your feet) and place one ankle on the other ankle. Push yourself towards the space behind you to stretch your calf (the muscle that runs along the back of the leg below the knee).

Coaching Tip:

-Make sure that in every practice, you start with ballistic/dynamic stretches and end with static stretches. Do this along with your players to make sure that this is being done. Let us be honest, it is going to be good for your overall health and well-being too. **Lead by example.** Have relatively the same stretch routine before and after games, so that your team can be mentally focused and physically become ready for the game or practice.

Chapter 13

Juggling

Juggling for a soccer player should be done to develop your skills that are applicable on the field. **Though being able to do an "around-the-world" with a ball is glamorous and fun, it does not often carry over well to a game.** I have played with many players that were great jugglers, but had a terrible first touch and were relatively useless on the field. Therefore, make sure when you juggle, its purpose is to become better with your in-game abilities. Otherwise, if you would prefer to be a freestyler (juggler), then this information does not apply to you. For most of the readers of this book that are looking to become better defenders, midfielders, forwards, or goalies, juggling is a way to have touches on the ball and to be able to use the top side of your foot.

When juggling, be sure to juggle the ball so that it either has no spin or a bit of backspin to make it easier for you to juggle. Putting forward spin on the ball makes it so that you constantly have to reach for the ball, to make sure that your foot is underneath the ball. Additionally, make sure to emphasize both feet, especially your opposite foot because a good soccer player is capable of using both feet. Developing only one foot will ensure a much more difficult career in this wonderful sport.

Next, when you practice juggling, do not be one of those people that tries to obtain a higher number of juggles using predominantly your thighs, as shown in the picture. The portion above your knees where you juggle the ball with your thighs is a portion of your body that you are very rarely going to use in a game. Therefore, practicing juggling with your thighs is spending quality practice time very inefficiently. Be logical and methodical about how you are trying to become better as a juggler because you want juggles to be similar to touches that you will be taking in a game. Use the top side of your foot to have an efficient first touch and better ability to settle the ball out of the air.

Parenting Tip:

-Ensure that when your child is juggling, they are using a goals-based approach. A goals-based approach means that your child should not just juggle to juggle. Have them set a goal for how many juggles they are looking to reach. Saying that "I want to juggle a lot for a long time" does not excite oneself. Increase their ability to juggle by having them say "I want to reach 65 juggles because my highest ever before was 60." **Having a measurable goal makes improvement much more realistic and something that your child's mind can work on achieving.** Therefore, set goals that are measurable where you can quickly determine if your child met his or her goal or not.

Coaching Tip:

-Something to keep in mind when your players are waiting in line for their turn to dribble through a set of cones or there is not currently any direction for the next drill in the practice is an ideal time for them to work on your juggling. **Standing with the ball at your feet without developing your skills is wasteful.** However, if you are alone by yourself with a soccer ball, you would be much better off working on your first touch, attacking with the ball, developing foot skills, or working on your shot. Waiting in line during a practice does not permit many other things to do with the ball other than juggling.

Chapter 14

Soccer Mindset

In soccer and in life, you can do whatever you put your mind to as long as you have the action to back up your decision. To be a useful player, it is imperative that you do not carry any limiting beliefs. It is essential that the ideas that you tell yourself fully align with the person and player that you want to be. **Examples of limiting beliefs are "I am not good with my left foot," "I cannot score," or "I am not that fast."** A simple change in mindset and some follow-up action make a massive difference in a player's career.

Do not ever say that you have a "weak foot." If you are not as good with your left foot, call it your "opposite foot," so you have a "strong foot" and an "opposite foot." Also, saying that "I am not fast" will pretty much ensure that you never become fast. Keep in mind, as discussed in other chapters, that being a fast soccer player is as much about your first touch and your ability to control the ball as it is about you being able to sprint without the ball. Sure, you may never get to the point to where you are winning 50-yard sprints against Usain Bolt, but limiting yourself from the beginning by saying that you are not fast will make it so that you never become fast. It ensures that you do not do the steps of squatting, deadlifting, sprinting, and additional training that allows you to become faster.

Furthermore, telling yourself that "I cannot score" and "I am not good at scoring" will make it so that you do not seek out the knowledge and the information that teaches you how to become a good scorer. Reading the books and watching the videos to become better is an efficient way to cut your learning curve and become better really quickly. Anytime you go to play soccer, on any team, there is always going to be people that can play defense and midfield. However, a person that can consistently score is uncommon. Knowing that you can score will give you so much confidence in your game that you would never want to limit your mindset by saying that you cannot do one of the most essential things in the game.

There are many more limiting beliefs in the game than the ones mentioned previously, such as your size, your height, or your newness to the sport. **Make sure that anything that holds you back within your mind, you reframe in a way that will make you better and strive for greatness.** Therefore, you may not be as good with your opposite foot as you want to be, but it will help to rephrase it as "I am working to get there. I will be there with knowledge, time, and persistence." Say "I may not currently a fast runner, but that does not keep me from being a fast soccer player nor does that keep me from training to become a faster runner, while gaining the knowledge to do so." Say "though I do not score many goals currently in a game, I will work to gain information of tips, tricks, and tactics to take better shots, to beat more defenders, and shoot with more accuracy and power.

Parenting Tip:

-Being around other negative players can make your child a bit more negative too. Let us be honest, we have all played with that other person or have a child that has played with another child that plays only for themselves and anything that goes wrong, they blame everyone else. They are counterproductive to the goals of the team, so try to work with your child to help improve their mindset. Keep up your positivity, work to have other people to be positive, and encourage others around you, including your son or daughter. **Guard yourself, guard your mind, and guard your child's mind against the negative people that are on his or her team.**

Coaching Tip:

-Make sure that your players remove any negative thoughts as they come to them. On the field or off, you want to make sure that if people are telling you their limiting beliefs, do not become mad at them. **Becoming mad will make it worse.** Your teammate feels like you will be patronizing or condescending them if you try to correct their mindsets. Instead, let them know that you used to be that way too.

Say "I used to have limiting beliefs which held me back. They made it so that it took me longer to become the player I wanted to be, but all I did was change my mindset while implementing more actions. As a result, I was able to become the player that I truly wanted to be. I am not perfect either, but with a few modifications in your mindset and your form, you will be a great soccer player too!"

Bonus!

Wouldn't it be nice to have the steps in this book on an easy 1-page printout for you to take to the field? Well, here is your chance!

Go to this Link for an **Instant** 1-Page Printout: UnderstandSoccer.com/free-printout.

This FREE guide is simply a "Thank You" for purchasing this book. This 1-page printout will ensure that the knowledge you obtain from this book makes it to the field.

Free Book?

How would you like to obtain the next book in the series for free and receive it before anyone else?

Join the Soccer Squad Book Team today and receive your next book (and potentially future books) for FREE.

Signing up is easy and does not cost anything.

Check out this website for more information:

UnderstandSoccer.com/soccer-squad-book-team

Thank You for Reading!

Dear Reader,

I hope you enjoyed and learned from ***Soccer Training: A Step-by-Step Guide on 14 Topics for Intelligent Soccer Players, Coaches, and Parents***. I truly enjoyed writing these steps and tips to ensure you improve your game, your team's game, or your child's game.

When I was writing this book and having others take a look at it, I received some great insights on the book. As an author, I love feedback. Candidly, you are the reason that I wrote this book and plan to write more. Therefore, tell me what you liked, what you loved, what can be improved, and even what you hated. I'd love to hear from you. Visit UnderstandSoccer.com and scroll to the bottom of the homepage to leave me a message in the contact section or email me at Dylan@UnderstandSoccer.com.

Finally, I need to ask a favor. I'd love and truly appreciate a review of ***Soccer Training: A Step-by-Step Guide***.

As you likely know, reviews are a key part of my process to see whether you, the reader, enjoyed my book. The reviews allow me to write more books and to continue to write articles on the UnderstandSoccer.com website. You have the power to help make or break my book. Please take the 2 minutes needed to leave a review on Amazon.com at https://www.amazon.com/gp/product-review/1717175058.

Thank you so much for reading ***Soccer Training: A Step-by-Step Guide*** and for spending time with me to understand soccer.

In gratitude,

Dylan Joseph

Glossary

50-50 - When a ball is passed into pressure or cleared up the field and your teammate and a player on the opposing team each have an equal (50%) chance of taking possession of the soccer ball.

Attacking Touch - Pushing the ball into space with your first touch, which is the opposite of taking a touch where the ball stops underneath you (at your feet).

Ball Hawk - Someone usually close to the ball, in the right place at the right time, and a person who specializes in scoring rebounds.

Bat - The bone (hardest portion) of your foot.

Bent/Curved Shot - A shot that spins and curves as it goes towards the net. This shot is used when you need to shoot around defenders or goalkeepers. Though you use the bone of your foot to strike the ball instead of following through the ball with your entire body, you just follow through with your leg and cross your legs after shooting the ball.

Bicycle Kick ("Overhead Kick") - where the ball is above you and you proceed to jump up and kick the ball over your body while the ball is in the air.

Broom - In this book, it is the area on your foot towards your toes. There is space in your shoe between your toes where there is a lot more fabric and a lot less bone, which makes it a soft area on your foot, similar to the softness of a broom.

Champions League - The UEFA Champions League is an annual soccer competition involving the best of the best club teams from many of the professional leagues in Europe.

Chop - This is performed with the outside of your foot. The leg that is cutting the ball must step entirely past the ball. Then, allow the ball to hit that leg/foot, which effectively stops the ball.

Having the ball stop next to your foot enables the ball to be pushed in a different direction quickly.

Counterattack ("Fast Break") - When the team defending gains possession of the ball and quickly travels up the field with the objective of taking a quick shot, so few of the other team's players can travel back to defend in time.

Crossbar Challenge - Played by one or more people where you attempt to hit the crossbar by shooting the ball from the 18-yard box.

Cruyff - Cut the ball, but leave yourself between the defender and the ball. In essence, you are cutting the ball behind your plant leg.

Cut - This is performed with the inside of your foot. The leg that is cutting the ball must step entirely past the ball. Then, allow the ball to hit that leg/foot, which effectively stops the ball. Having the ball stop next to your foot enables the ball to be pushed in a different direction quickly. Additionally, you may cut the ball so that it is immediately moving in the direction that you want to go.

Driven Shot - A shot struck with the bone of your foot, where you follow through with your entire body without crossing your legs. This is the most powerful type of shot.

Finishing - The purpose of shooting, which is to score.

Flick - Barely touching the ball to change the direction of the ball slightly for a teammate when a pass is being played to you.

Half-Volley - Striking the ball just after it hit the ground, but while the ball is still in the air.

Jab Step ("Feint," "Body Feint," "Fake," "Fake and Take," or "Shoulder Drop") - When you pretend to push the ball in one direction, but purposely miss, then plant with the foot that you missed the ball with to push the ball in the other direction.

Jockeying - When defending, backpedaling to maintain proper position in relation to the person attacking with the ball. When jockeying, the defender does not dive in for the ball. He or she waits for the ideal time to steal the ball or poke it away.

Jump Turn - Instead of pulling the ball back with the bottom of your foot, as you would do in the V pull back, stop the ball with the bottom of your foot as you jump past the ball, landing with both feet at the same time on the other side of the ball. Landing with both feet at the same time on the other side of the ball allows you to explode away in the direction from which you came.

Offside - When you pass the ball to a player on your team who is past the opposing team's last defender at the moment the kick is initiated. You cannot be offside on a throw-in or when you are on your own half of the field.

One-Time Shot - When a pass or cross is played to you and your first touch is a shot on net.

Opposite Foot - Your non-dominant foot. Out of your two feet, it is the one that you are not as comfortable using.

Outside of the Foot Shot ("Trivela") - Shooting with the bone of your foot where your toe is pointed down and in. The ball makes contact with the outside portion/bone of your foot. This shot is useful because it is quicker than a driven shot, it can provide bend like a bent shot, and is more powerful than a pass shot.

Pass Fake - Faking a pass. Keep your form the same as when you pass, including: 1) Looking at a teammate before you do a pass fake 2) Raise your passing leg high enough behind your body, so that an opponent believes you are going to kick the ball.

Pass Shot ("Finesse Shot") - A shot on the net using the inside of your foot to increase your accuracy. However, land past the ball on the follow through to increase the shot's power, similar to a shot taken with the bone of your foot.

Passing Lane - An area on the field where a teammate can pass you the ball directly, while the ball remains on the ground.

Pitch - A soccer field.

Rainbow - When you place one foot in front of the ball and the laces of the other foot behind the ball. Pin the ball between your feet and flick the ball up behind your body and over your head.

Roll ("Rollover") - Using the bottom of the toes of your foot, roll the ball parallel to the defender, crossing your feet when you plant. Then, bring your other foot around to uncross your feet and push the ball forward. The path the ball takes is the shape of an "L."

Self-Pass ("L," "Iniesta," or "La Croqueta") - Passing the ball from one foot to the other while running. Imagine you are doing a roll, but without your foot going on top of the ball. Instead, it is an inside of the foot pass from one foot and an inside of the foot push up the field with the other foot.

Set Piece ("Dead Ball") - A practiced plan used when the ball goes out of bounds or a foul is committed to put the ball back into play. The most common set pieces are throw-ins and free kicks.

Scissor - When the foot closest to the ball goes around the ball as you are attacking in a game. Emphasize turning your hips to fake the defender. To easily turn your hips, plant past the ball with your foot that is not going around the ball so that you can use the momentum of the moving ball to your advantage.

Shielding - Placing your body between the ball and the defender. With your back facing the defender and your arms wide, prevent him or her from traveling to the ball.

Shot Fake - Faking a shot. Make sure your form looks the same as when you shoot, including: 1) Looking at the goal before you do a shot fake 2) Arms out 3) Raise your shooting leg high enough behind your body, so it looks like you are going to shoot.

Square to your Teammate - Pointing your hips at a teammate.

Step On Step Out - In order to change direction, step on the ball with the bottom of your foot. Then, with the same foot that stepped on the ball, take another step to plant to the side of the ball, so that your other leg can come through and push the ball in a different direction.

Step Over - When you are next to the ball and you have your furthest leg from the ball step over the ball, so your entire body turns as if you are going in a completely different direction. The step over is best used along a sideline.

Through Ball/Run - When a pass is played into space in front of you, allowing you to continue your forward momentum.

Toe Poke/Toe Blow - Striking the ball with your big toe. The toe poke is the quickest shot, but often the most inaccurate shot.

Upper 90 - Either of the top corners on a net (corners are 90 degrees).

V Pull Back - Pull the ball backward using the bottom of your foot. Then, use your other leg to push the ball and accelerate forward in the other direction, hence the "V" in the V pull back.

Volley - Striking the ball out of the air before it hits the ground.

Wall Passing ("1-2 Passing") - A wall pass is when you pass it to a teammate and they pass it back to you with one touch similar to if you were to pass a ball against a wall.

Acknowledgments

I would like to thank you, the reader. I am grateful to provide you value and to help continue your journey of becoming a better and more confident soccer player, soccer coach, or soccer parent. Honestly, I am happy to serve you and thank you so much for the opportunity to do so. Also, I would like to acknowledge a few people in my life that have truly made a difference and have paved the way for me to share this knowledge with the world:

First, I want to start off with my wife. She is both beautiful inside and out, and I am fortunate and blessed to be able to share my life with her. I wish for both of our continued growth and an abundant relationship. Likewise, I appreciate all her feedback on improvements to this book.

Second, I would like to thank my sister who, though she is younger than me, I look up to her for her ability to be positive around negative people and situations. She is someone that even in the worst of circumstances keeps a level head, a calm demeanor, and looks for the silver lining. Furthermore, by implementing the skills mentioned in this book through hours of practice, she was able to be on the Varsity Girls' soccer team as a freshman at one of the largest high schools in the state. Furthermore, I appreciate all her suggestions on improvements to this book.

Third, I would like to acknowledge my mother, who has been a role model for what can be done when you put your mind to something and work hard towards your goals. Her work ethic and ability to overcome adversity are truly admirable, and I look up to her for this. Additionally, I appreciate all her feedback on using stronger wording and many grammatical improvements to this book.

Fourth, I would like to thank my father for always guiding me in the right direction towards God. I look up to him in many ways. I am glad that I was able to have such a great male role model in my life, which is something that so many other people do not have.

Lastly, I would like to thank my soccer mentor, Aaron Byrd, whose wisdom and soccer smarts have turned me into the player I am today. His guidance and knowledge about this awesome game have made it so that I can successfully pass this knowledge on to rising stars, coaches looking to improve their understanding of soccer, and caring parents!

Many thanks,

Dylan Joseph

What's Next?

Each of the chapters in this book peels back some of the layers in the different areas a soccer player can improve. Implementing the guides, tips, and tricks you just read in this book will help you become an "overnight sensation." If you enjoyed the contents of this book, please visit me at UnderstandSoccer.com to let me know what you were most excited to read.

I aim to create a book on nearly every topic covered by each chapter and would love for you to answer the **one question poll** at UnderstandSoccer.com/poll to help me in determining what area of soccer you want to improve next. Your vote on the upcoming books in the series will help determine what book is to follow!

Made in the USA
Lexington, KY
11 May 2019